Waves of WONDER

WRITTEN BY
KEVIN & LATOYA STALLWORTH

M₁
T

LOVE,
YOU HAVE GIVEN
LEARNED AND MATURED
YOUR CLASS, EVEN IN SO SHORT OF
TIME! WE ESPECIALLY APPRECIATE
YOU BLESSING US AND VISITING US
DURING JOURNEY'S HOSPITAL
STAY. IT MEANT SO
MUCH. WE
HOPE YOU
FIND THIS
BOOK TO BE A
"FUN READ" DURING
YOUR HOLIDAY
BREAK. ENJOY
THE WAVES
OF WONDER!

—KEVIN & LATOYA
STALLWORTH

Copyright © 2017 by Kevin & Latoya Stallworth

Published by Faithwalk Harvest Center
P.O. Box 771
Carpentersville, IL 60110
Email: info@faithwalkharvestctr.org

Waves of Wonder

ISBN: 978-0-9973757-3-2
Printed in the United States of America

Book Cover Designed By First Class Media Designs

TABLE OF CONTENTS

Dedication

Foreword

Introduction

Chapter 1 - Waves of Service

Chapter 2 - Waves of Food

Chapter 3 - Waves of Entertainment

Chapter 4 - Waves of Destinations

Chapter 5 - Waves of Nations

Chapter 6 - Waves of Shops

Chapter 7 - Waves of Grandeur

Chapter 8 - Waves of Relaxation

Chapter 9 - Waves of Care

Chapter 10 - Waves of Financial Preparation

Chapter 11 – Waves of Good-Byes

Waves from the Heart

DEDICATION

We thank and praise God for this vision to share what He has blessed us to experience for ten years!

We dedicate this book to our parents for raising us with a Godly foundation. We are grateful for their unfailing love, guidance and support!

We dedicate this book to our daughter Journey who has her own experience on the "waves of wonder" at a young age. We also dedicate this book to our friends Colleen (aka "Irish Granny") and Zoe for joining us on our adventures after hearing our story!

This book is in memory of our mother, Sylvia Stallworth, our sister Audrey Blye and our grandmother Marguerite Thomas. We know they are happy for us!

FOREWORD

"YES!" was the word that filled the room on June 6, 2006. We were now engaged and our wedding planning had started. Shortly afterward we had the wedding date, the colors, the bridal party, the reception hall and the church confirmed. The only thing that was uncertain was where we would spend our honeymoon. A few weeks before the big day our frustration was overheard by a co-worker. Without hesitation he confidently gave us a recommendation. Initially we thought, "No way! Who wants to be in the middle of nowhere with nothing to do? The constant rocking and swaying will make us sick and our entire honeymoon will be ruined." After researching we said, "It doesn't seem to be so bad. Why not? Let's try it. If we don't like it we have the rest of our lives to try other adventures."

Our honeymoon itinerary was finally confirmed, and on the day after our wedding we were on our way. We were in awe of the amazing adventure as we traveled to our destination and back. We decided that from then on, we would choose this adventure every year to celebrate our anniversary. We couldn't wait to tell our family and friends about what we experienced.

In 2015, during our eighth anniversary vacation, we were discussing the fact that we were as amazed as we were the first year. In the midst of our discussion God gave us a vision to write a book that would encourage others around the world to experience the wonders we have experienced.

From that moment we prayed and started writing. Daily we received more and more confirmation to move ahead. After months of planning and writing we began to run with the vision for Waves of Wonder in anticipation of our tenth wedding anniversary on 7-7-17!

Introduction

"Home Sweet Home" is usually what you say when you return to your permanent residence. However, when the attendant swipes our cards and ushers us onto the platform to start our vacation, "Home Sweet Home" are the first words that come out of our mouths. At that time our expectation is already set and we are ready to enjoy the wonders ahead.

There are 365 days in a year and most Americans work 250 of those days. In addition to careers, we all have to deal with various responsibilities each day, leading to busy or even stressful lifestyles. Taking at least a week each year to relax and unwind from daily routines is vital if we are to maintain healthy and balanced lives.

Unfortunately, some people's vacation experiences end up being almost as stressful as their daily routines. In many cases, vacations involve staying in hotels in unfamiliar areas, struggling to find out how to navigate to various points of interest, trying to find decent restaurants within a reasonable distance, and constantly spending money (usually more money than budgeted for).

Do you ever wish to avoid this kind of stress when you vacation? If so, there is a vacation in which all of the entertainment venues, all of the restaurants and all of the places to relax are literally "down the hallway" from the place where you spend the night. You do not have to worry about spending money for each little activity every day. After paying a "one time" fee, just about everything on the vacation is covered in advance, helping you to easily stay within your budget.

What kind of vacation is this? None other than a cruise vacation! Nothing can compare to leaving the land and escaping to the ocean where you can be restored and rejuvenated. Everyone should try cruising for themselves. This is not your ordinary vacation. It is truly one of the best vacations a person can experience!

Chapter 1

Waves of Service

Service has always been important to us. While courting each other we learned how our daily decisions were centered on service. During our marriage counseling we discovered how important acts of service were for both of us. As we were wedding planning we decided to have our reception at a banquet hall that displayed great service several years before.

Deciding which dealership we purchased our first car from was based on the service we received. As we were researching daycare centers for our daughter Journey, we were drawn to the service that we received. There is an endless amount of service offered to people daily which draws billions of people back.

As we were making arrangements for our honeymoon we were struck by the excellent service we received over the phone while we were booking our very first cruise. We were informed about all of our choices such as where we wanted to cruise, what type of ship we were interested in, what type of stateroom we wanted and what part of the ship we preferred. We were also given the choice of what time we preferred for dinner and how many people we desired at our dinner table.

Once we were booked we received information about everything we needed to do before and upon arriving. A few days before leaving we received luggage tags in the mail with our stateroom numbers on them. These tags were to be put on our luggage once we arrived at the port, so that our luggage would be delivered right to our stateroom door.

We were able to book our airfare through the cruise line which guaranteed our arrival at the ship even if the plane was delayed. Once we arrived at the airport we were greeted by friendly staff who directed us to our airport transfer to the port. At the port our luggage was carried out by the porters, and then we proceeded in line (according to our last name) for check-in. At the end of the check-in process we were again greeted by friendly staff and were provided key cards which allowed us access to our staterooms.

Once we departed from check-in we were greeted by photographers who were eager to capture the moment with various props and of course the famous life buoy. The entire boarding process was well organized. We were just in awe to see how thousands of arriving people knew exactly what to do without much hustle and frustration.

Crossing over from land to the ship was just the beginning of what was ahead for the week. Once we were on the ship smiling faces, music and eyes of amazement brought forth a mindset of relaxation as we smiled back thinking, "WOW! We're on vacation!" What has been so amazing is that after years of cruising this same greeting has continued and has brought back the same feeling each year.

Once on board we were informed that lunch was being served. At the entrance to the dining area we quickly snapped pictures of the world's greatest fruit carving which stated "WELCOME." There were also amazing bread carvings all around. Then to our surprise there were huge ice carvings throughout the dining area. We filled our stomachs with various types of food, desserts, and fruits. Then, after more food, desserts and fruits we were ready to check out our stateroom. As we arrived at the door and swiped our keycard we opened up to our stateroom for the next week. We were greeted with a swan made out of towels on our bed and an itinerary to inform us of the evening activities planned.

We enjoyed unpacking our luggage and putting our items away in the closets and drawers provided in our stateroom. Soon afterward we were greeted by our stateroom attendant who informed us of what services would be provided to make sure our stateroom was kept just the way we wanted it. As we sat on the bed and looked around we thought, "Wow! We're in for the time of our lives!" Finally after a year of wedding planning, working and serving others we had landed in a place where we were about to be taken care of. We had no idea what we had stepped into.

The service that we received and continue to receive each year has been astonishing. If there is a need at any time, a friendly, passionate staff member is right there to assist you. It just truly brought joy to our hearts to witness and experience a vacation where the staff goes out of their way to accommodate our every need. During our cruises we form great relationships with the staff who take care of us on a daily basis. We found ourselves in the presence of people who genuinely care and truly want to make the experience the best that you've had. Every year we look forward to meeting our stateroom attendant, waiter and assistant waiter. The impact that they have on our lives in just one week leaves footprints in our hearts. Service is truly key. It is maintained well throughout our cruise vacations.

Chapter 2

Waves of Food

We've all experienced the late night hunger. After you've had dinner and dessert you still have a taste for something a few hours later. You end up going down to your kitchen looking for some chips, ice cream, fruit or drink because there's nothing quite like satisfying the late night hunger. While cruising we were astonished when we learned food was available 24 hours.

In the previous chapter we mentioned that once we were on board we were welcomed to eat in the dining area for lunch. This lunch is like no other! There is a buffet-style lunch that's unending. We're not just talking about a typical hamburger, fries and soda. There's an array of meats, sides, vegetables, soups, salads and fruits to meet the appetites of everyone.

Of course after you've had as many plates as you desire there are desserts such as cakes, pies, cheesecakes, puddings, parfaits, and cookies. There are several beverage stations around, but don't worry. If your hands are too full, before you know it you'll be greeted by a committed dining staff member who will say, "What would you like to drink and how many?" Again, the service is compared to none.

The staff takes care of you with passionate, committed and friendly service.

After leaving lunch we were informed of our dinner location. We were given the option of having dinner in the formal dining room or we could go back for the buffet style dinner (the same place we had lunch). We decided to check out the formal dining room. Once we arrived we were seated at our assigned table and introduced to our waiter and assistant waiter who would be serving us for the next week. First we were offered bread and then we were asked our beverage preference. Shortly after we were given an explanation of the dinner theme, our waiter gave recommendations while allowing us time to look over the menu. Soon we were greeted by the eager photographers to capture another great memory. Once our order was placed we enjoyed a delicious appetizer followed by an outstanding presentation of dinner and a delicious entrée.

After dinner our table was cleaned off and crumbs swept as we were handed our dessert menu. After indulging in dessert we were offered coffee. The waiter informed us of the dinner theme for the next night. The waiter also reminded us of the formal night which would consist of lobster and steak later in the week. We just could not wait to see what else was in store!

Later in the evening we found out from our itinerary that we could order room service with several items at anytime. After a few days of cruising we decided to try it. We placed a midnight order and a few minutes before midnight there came a knock at the door with our "late night meal". We just laughed, thinking, "This is unbelievable! What have we done to deserve this great vacation and such great service?" Another time, we ordered breakfast and there was another knock on the door a few minutes before our requested delivery time. It was such a magnificent moment when we sat on our balcony looking out into the middle of the ocean enjoying breakfast together without rushing to get dressed and go down to the dining area.

Each year as we cruised we found different places to eat on the ship (depending on what ship we were on). One ship had a small restaurant that opened at 9pm each night and they provided fried chicken, tacos, smoothies, and salads until 4am. During this cruise we often found ourselves craving chicken and salads after 9pm. Another ship had pizza and deli sandwiches offered throughout the night if we weren't interested in the room service menu. Again during this cruise we found ourselves craving pizza and deli sandwiches after 9pm. After nine great years we found this to be one of the greatest times together and we truly look forward to this aspect of our cruise every year.

What's vacation without ice cream? At the poolside you are able to enjoy ice cream from the ice cream machine. People of all ages line up to twist their favorite flavor into a cone while smiling as they walk back to the pool area for more fun and relaxation. The first year we took our daughter on a cruise her eyes lit up when we walked over to the ice cream machine (a heartfelt moment that we shared).

In 2015 we were given the opportunity to tour the galley. During this tour we saw where the dinner was cooked and received by the waiter. This daily preparation takes several hours. In the galley there is a screen that informs the chefs exactly how many steaks, chicken, lobster, etc. to cook. This way food is not wasted and comes out fresh for each cruiser. Waiters have an assigned way of entering into the kitchen to make sure there are no traffic jams and fewer accidents while walking in and out of the galley. Once the food has been picked up the screen notifies the chef so they are aware of how much more food is needed.

When returning into the galley the waiter places the used dishes in marked racks to prepare for the dish washer. Some ships provide dinners for over 4,000 cruisers daily so everything in the galley is HUGE. We even witnessed how quickly bread is made through a special machine which forms 30 pieces of bread in seconds.

Truly we were amazed at how this all works in the galley. The purpose of the operations in the galley is to make sure that we as "cruisers" are able to sit back and enjoy the great food and excellent service throughout the ship.

Every year we cruise we look forward to filling our stomachs with familiar and unfamiliar foods. It's such a great experience because you have so many opportunities to try different foods. Of course if you don't like it you're not charged. There is always a friendly staff member to offer you something else, or more of the same.

There are specialty dining venues and shops where you can purchase food for an additional charge at your own discretion. Aboard the ship everyone's hunger will be satisfied every second, minute, and hour of each day. Eat away! You're on vacation.

Chapter 3

Waves of Entertainment

There are many words one can use in describing a cruise vacation. However, "boring" is not one of them. There is so much to do on board the ship that it is literally impossible to finish the cruise and say that you have experienced everything! From the minute we settle on board, we receive our itinerary so that we can find the activities that catch our attention.

From the very first evening, we realized that the theatrical and musical performances on cruise lines are second-to-none. We were enamored by the stellar performances of the actors, actresses and singers in the nightly shows and concerts. We can't help but keep our eyes on the live orchestra that accompanies each production with dynamic, skilled musicality. The sets, backdrops and "props" for the shows are so well structured that they mentally transport us to the intended setting of the story. The cruise productions are just as classy as any that we've seen in the world-class theater district of Chicago!

During our cruise vacation, we attend just about every show that is offered at the theater. We attend the comedy shows, magic shows, and the game shows. We've even sat in the theater to watch some of our fellow cruisers enjoy a competitive game of BINGO.

More than likely, your cruise vacation will have tropical destinations (unless you cruise to Alaska or another "far-northern" destination). When you are headed to the tropics, ice is probably the last thing on your mind. However, we have even skated in the ship's ice rink on some of our vacations! We love to go to the ice show, where ice cast puts on an exciting skating performance which incorporates popular music, dazzling choreography and daring acrobatics.

Though we are not gamblers, we realized very early on that the casino is a major venue on every ship. We often pass through the casino when walking from one end of the ship to the other, observing our fellow cruisers taking small (or large) risks with their money in hopes of cashing in big!

We love good movies. Therefore we couldn't believe our eyes when we looked at the layout of one of our ships and found out that a movie theater was on board. At the designated time, we went to the theater and sat in stadium seating under dimmed lights and enjoyed a movie. In the near future, we look forward to cruising on one of the ships that offers the IMAX theater experience.

In the evenings, when we traverse the ship from one end to the other, we often hear individual passengers singing on microphones to soundtracks of popular songs. Yes, Karaoke is a major part of the cruise experience!

Since we have no obligation to get up early for work during our cruise week, we love to stay up late. On many late nights we walk around the ship for a late night snack or to go somewhere to sit down, relax and enjoy the peaceful atmosphere. Even after we retreat to our stateroom, the cruise ship remains very much alive – even into the early morning hours. The many clubs, bars, and lounges on board are popular with the thousands guests who enjoy the night life on the high seas.

No vacation is complete without taking a dip in the swimming pool. In our cruise vacations, we do not make exception to this rule. From the earliest moments of the cruise, our daughter Journey persistently and continually asks, "When can we go swimming? When can we go swimming?" So, at our very earliest opportunity the three of us immerse ourselves in the cooling waters of the pool surrounded by the smiling faces of swimmers, sunbathers and people-watchers. We love the Caribbean sounds of the live band that usually plays by the poolside. When we've had enough of the water, we usually get a scoop of ice cream or a virgin piña colada from one of the stands near the pool. We enjoy relaxing on a pool chair in the warmth of the beautiful sun. On Journey's first cruise she discovered the "splash area" specifically geared for children her age. She enjoys swimming and going to slide down the water slide.

On our "sea days" (when the ship does not dock at a port), we have time to go up to the sports deck. As a family, we enjoy recreational activities on the sports deck, such as playing mini-golf. We also enjoy inline skating, rock climbing, zip-lining and riding the waves of the flow rider. A full basketball court sits in the middle of the sports deck which is always filled with young men (and even some young women) "hooping it up" – that is, until the staff transforms the court in preparation for the cruise's competitive volleyball tournament!

On a couple of our cruises, we have had consultations with fitness trainers. Yes! You can receive fitness training, and you can work out in the ship's state-of-the art fitness center! When we get the resolve to go to the fitness center, we usually jog side by side on the treadmill while listening to inspiring worship songs on our headphones. On other days, we choose to do our jogging (or walking) on the beautiful jogging track that stretches from end-to-end of the upper deck of the ship.

On the last night of the cruise there is a "finale" show in the theater featuring singing, dancing and other forms of entertainment. We never miss this exciting experience which features a parade of the cruise staff – including chefs, waiters, stateroom attendants, entertainment staff, and many of the executive officials, and sometimes even the captain – marching on stage and singing us a "farewell" song.

After all of the festivities, fun and fitness, you'll also agree that there is not one moment when you would be able to say that you are bored!

Chapter 4

Waves of Destinations

"Aruba, Jamaica, ooh I want to take you to Bermuda, Bahama, come on pretty Mama. Key Largo, Montego, baby why don't we go"... This song by the Beach Boys has a prominent meaning in our lives. Our yearly cruises have made it possible for us to sing along, knowing that we've been to every one of those places!

One of the things that really sets a cruise vacation above any other vacation is the fact that you can visit many different nations in a single trip. As you travel between destinations on the cruise, you are either resting in your stateroom or you are having fun participating in one of the many exciting activities on the ship. Sure, people have taken multi-nation trips by means other than cruising. However, such trips likely involve the tedious experience of packing and unpacking for a monotonous ride on a car, bus, train or plane between each destination.

The cruise industry is a major economic blessing to almost every nation in which the ships dock. The natives at each destination gladly anticipate the arrival of the ships because they know that the cruise passengers will support the local economy by touring their cities, eating in their restaurants and buying goods and souvenirs from local stores. There are nations that we would never have even thought to visit had it not been for the cruise ports there.

The cruise line sponsors excursions at every destination. Though the cruise line offers adventurous excursions such as diving, snorkeling, zip-lining, swimming with dolphins, etc. we usually decide to take cruise-sponsored tours of the island or city. On our tours, we have many exciting memories. We have climbed the Queen's Staircase in Nassau, Bahamas. We have viewed coral reefs from a semi-submarine in Cozumel, Mexico. We have ridden in a horse-drawn carriage in historic Belize City. We have visited the turtle farm in Grand Cayman. We have watched rafters on the peaceful Martha Brae River in Jamaica. We have stepped into the beautiful blue Caribbean waters of Roatan, Honduras. We have been to The Mountain Top in St. Thomas, Virgin Islands. We have almost touched the low-flying jets landing at the runway next to Maho Beach in St. Maarten. We have purchased lovely crafts from the people of Antigua. We have viewed the lush Piton peaks in St. Lucia. We have taken photographs on the shores of Bathsheba Beach in Barbados. We have walked the streets of Basseterre to experience the local culture of St. Kitts. We have built sandcastles at Blue Bay in

Curacao. We have climbed to the top of the Casibari Rock Formations in Aruba. We have viewed the dazzling pink sand beaches of Bermuda. We have even kick backed, relaxed and enjoyed a beach-side barbecue in Haiti.

We count it a great blessing, not only to be able to visit the various nations ourselves, but to also take our daughter with us to experience different nations and cultures. The memories of visiting these nations will be beneficial to her when she hears about them on the news and on the internet, and when she studies about them in social studies and geography classes in the future.

As we look ahead to our future cruise vacations, we expect to experience cruises in the Mediterranean, in Northern Europe, and in Asia (in addition to visiting all of the islands we have not yet been to in the Caribbean).

So, to where do you dream of traveling? I assure you, the most exciting way to get there is in a cruise ship!

Chapter 5

Waves of Nationalities

We love to get to know people of all backgrounds, races, and cultures. Therefore, it was to our great delight that each year, we get the chance to experience first-class service from people from all over the world.

In this modern world, the word "diversity" has become a key objective in many facets of society. The cruise industry is a clear leader in the area of diversity. At least 40 nations are represented among the staff on most cruises. Sometimes up to 80 nations are represented. On every cruise, we have seen and spoken with staff members from all over Europe, Africa, Asia, Australia, South America, Central America, the Caribbean, Mexico, Canada and of course the United States of America!

We will never forget the child-like amazement we felt on our first cruise when a waiter took almost twenty minutes out of his schedule to tell us about his native country. His name tag identified his country of origin (as do the name tags of all cruise staff members). We had never heard of that country before, so we decided to ask him about that nation. Instead of giving us a hurried answer and moving on to another work duty, the kind gentleman was actually overjoyed to stop and give us details about his country. He even went on to talk about his life experiences in that country. In that moment, we were honored to become educated about a foreign land, and we obtained a desire to visit that country in the future.

The international presence of the cruise staff truly helps us embrace the fact that the world is much bigger than our beloved homeland of the U.S.A. No matter what our cruise itineraries have been, we are always thrilled to experience the gracious hospitality of cultures from every corner of the globe. Their service, their creativity, their knowledge, their kindness, and their genuine joy in spending time with us makes them worthy of our honor and gratitude. Therefore, we are mindful to always give them the only fitting response, which is, "Shakar", "Xiexie", "Bedankt", "Merci", "Danke", "Dhanyavaad", "Grazie", "Salamat", "Kansha", "Gamsa", "Dzieki", "Gracias", "Tesekkurler", or simply, "Thank you very much!'

Chapter 6

Waves of Shops

"Postcards, key chains, and t-shirts O my!" What's a vacation without shopping? Souvenirs are all over the place. If you're on the ship there are on-board shops and if you're at port there's port shopping. While on board you have opportunities to shop. There are quick convenient stores to purchase items you may have forgotten to pack. There are stores which sell everything from jackets to magnets. Throughout the ship you can find jewelry stores with stunning diamonds and pearls. Of course for the ladies there are some name brand purse stores which have a variety of stylish bags, wallets, and sunglasses just to name a few. For the men there are watches, caps, and sporting equipment among other items.

Throughout the week several one day sales are held. During this time large tables of items are set up right outside or inside the store. Cruisers gather around before the sale starts to get ready to grab whatever their hearts desire. You can find great prices on items for your entire family, friends, co-workers and others for whom you may want to make purchases.

Of course Journey found a shop which catered to her needs of dolls, stuffed animals, and other trinkets. After a few days of scoping out what she wanted she finally made a purchase of a glittery silver wallet for only $10. Then, a few aisles down, she was overtaken by the sight of a purple stuffed monkey which hangs off her neck. She was overjoyed when she was able to purchase wooden carved crayons from Aruba for her preschool teacher. This was another moment that captured our heart!

The shops are open at various times and you can usually find them open until early in the morning during at-sea days. If you enjoy specialty foods you can often find well known coffee shops, cupcake shops, and ice-cream shops on the ship as well.

While at the port we normally book an excursion which includes shopping. We are taken to well-known areas in town to suit our shopping desires. Months prior to our vacation we set-up a budget (which we will discuss in a later chapter) for our times of shopping during the cruise week. This way we are not easily swayed to overspend and purchase excessively.

There are always markets near where the ship docks. At those markets bargaining is often done. Therefore, we are able to bless others with souvenirs upon our return. Every year we think of someone who we want to unexpectedly bless. We are always on a mission to find that special keepsake. We have a special friend for whom we purchase a pen/pencil for every year. We are always eager to search for her gift. Every year we find ourselves under our budget after making our purchases. Again, there is something for everyone - even in the shopping wave!

Chapter 7

Waves of Grandeur

We must admit. When we reached the end of the gangway and we entered the ship on our first cruise, we did not know what we would see once inside. However, as soon as we entered the doors of the ship, we knew we had entered into luxury. Just a few steps past the main entryway was the main lobby of the ship, which included two beautiful winding staircases. The staircases were graced with beautiful brass railings which give off a golden glimmer when the light shines on them. Just behind the staircase were a set of glass elevators. The elevators reached so high that they appeared to launch the privileged vacationers into the very sky. A platform and a large grand piano sat at the bottom of the staircase. The balconies of several floors surrounded and overlooked this grand lobby. Before we could proceed anywhere else, we had to pause for a few minutes and marvel at the exquisite sight of the main lobby. We thought, "If this is only the first area of the ship we see, imagine what the rest of it looks like!"

As you may have guessed, the rest of the ship is just as fabulous! There is no more appropriate word with which we can describe the ship but by the word "grandeur." The word "grandeur" means "splendor and impressiveness, especially of appearance or style." Truly, every cruise ship we have sailed has been splendid and impressive. Even in our more recent cruises, as we make our way through the ships, we are taken aback by the creativity and artfulness by which the ships are designed. On some of the ships, there has been a large plaza area made to look like the "Town Square" of a city, surrounded by shops and eateries. On other ships, we were privileged to walk through gardens with artistic sculptures and ornamental features on our way to various activities on-board.

It is always an interesting experience the first time we have to navigate ourselves through the beautiful corridors to our stateroom. However, the cruise line already has tools in place to keep us from getting disoriented! There are huge electronic "way-finding" devices on the walls, in which we can simply input our stateroom number. The device then shows us the path to our stateroom. As we walk down the beautiful corridors, beautiful works of art lines the walls. Some of the artwork includes historic photos or sculptures. Some of it includes nostalgia from recent decades of pop-culture. We finally open the door to our "home sweet home" (our stateroom). A large comfortable bed sits in front of us. A dresser, a television, a cushion chair and a coffee table surround us. This assures us that we will feel as though we were in the master suite of our own home.

In 2016, Journey's eyes lit up with joy when the stateroom attendant pulled down a bunk bed from the ceiling just for her. The ladder for the bunk bed was pulled down, and Journey happily climbed up. What excitement filled her heart when she sat on her bunk and looked down at her parents who had stretched out on the bigger bed beneath her.

One of the grandest locations on the ship is the formal dining room. On most ships, the formal dining room is two or three stories tall, with an open area in the middle. Shiny wood paneling covers the walls and stately curtains grace the windows. A large, impressive chandelier hangs from the ceiling over the open area in the middle of the dining room. When we eat in the formal dining room, we can simply take a look at the design of the room and know that we are about to have one of the best dining experiences at sea or on land.

On some ships, we marvel at the use of Greco-Roman architecture (including large pillars, columns, etc.) in places such as the theater and spa. On other ships, we enjoy the atmosphere set by the neo-futuristic designs in the lobbies and lounges.

On any ship, prepare to be impressed! When you board the ship, you are transported into an atmosphere of luxury and unique artistry, and unsurpassed beauty. It is easy to forget that you are actually on a ship in the middle of the water! Like us, you may find yourself just pausing in the middle of the ship and saying, "Wow! I am simply in awe of what I see!"

Chapter 8

Waves of Relaxation

As professionals in human services and engineering we both know that self-care is important. Taking care of oneself is critical to survival as professionals and as people yet it is often neglected. It can be extremely challenging, especially while trying to balance careers, family, ministry and other various activities in your personal life. During our marriage counseling we discussed various ways to maintain our well-being. Before our wedding we made an agreement to make sure we enjoyed a yearly vacation together despite what may be going on in our lives.

In 2012 when our daughter was born we experienced the first challenge to this agreement. We pondered, "Should we go on vacation with our four-month old baby or should we stay home?" We reflected back on our agreement, discussed the importance of maintaining a healthy marriage and considered our support system (which included our parents). Our parents joyfully offered to take care of our young baby while we enjoyed our fifth anniversary. After we carefully considered the decision, we realized that we couldn't deny ourselves the opportunity to say "Home Sweet Home" to our yearly cruise vacation!

Once you are on board you are informed of various ways to relax while enjoying time away. On each ship you are guaranteed to find the spa where various services are offered. If you need a massage, book it. If you need a pedicure, book it. If you need a manicure, book it. If you need your hair styled, book it. If you need to just sit in the steam room, book it. If you're interested in going in as a couple or alone your needs will be met and you'll be drawn back each year. There is something at the spa for everyone to enjoy.

After enjoying time in the spa there are several "adult only" areas. These areas are quiet and off to the side. You can grab a chair and lie back as you read a good book, listen to music, meditate, sleep or just listen to the calming splash of the waves. There are hot tubs in this area as well. Many cruisers are seen there just relaxing and releasing from the cares of the world. Truly it is an experience where you can be free and not worry about answering the pohne, opening emails, responding to texts, running to the store, cooking dinner, or preparing for the next work day. You truly feel relieved!

After winding down at the "adult only" area you are right on time for a late night movie. On some ships you can walk right over to the pool deck and grab a chair and relax while watching a movie. Each day you can find which movies are playing in your itinerary. Depending on which ship you're on, if you don't want to be outside you can walk down the hall to the movie theater and catch a movie without trying to purchase a ticket. Just walk in, grab a seat, and "lights, camera action"!

If you are still looking for a way to relax the pool is usually open at night. You can walk over to one of several pools, take a swim, sit on the side and kick your feet or just lay on the pool chairs. You can do whatever you feel like doing. You're on vacation! There are even certain times when a poolside buffet is set up. You're welcome to grab a plate or (several plates) right at the pool. You are sure to find whatever brings you relaxation somewhere on the ship.

Making the time to take care of oneself is a personal decision. The lack of time is the most common excuse people give. The second most common is finances (which we will discuss in a later chapter). Seeing and experiencing the benefits of self-care can improve many aspects of a person's life and can result in a higher quality of life!

Chapter 9

Waves of Care

In 2015 we were extremely excited to take Journey with us for the first time. We were now ready to expose her to our cruise life. We eagerly prepared her by showing her pictures of the ship and explaining what cruising would be like.

On the ship Journey participated in the children's program. Children's programs are divided by age groups. Once you are onboard there is an orientation that informs you of the care that is available during the cruise.

The program offers parents a drop off option where their children are supervised by trained child-friendly professionals. If desired, children can stay for lunch and/or dinner depending on whether or not it is a port day. Some days the children are escorted down to a secluded part of the dining area or to one of the specialty shops to enjoy their desired foods and desserts.

In the children's program there are several rooms. Each room is set up with bright bold colors, consisting of child friendly furniture to accommodate each age group. Each day there is a theme and the children's activities are centered around that theme.

While there Journey engaged in arts and crafts, story time, painting, singing/dancing, playing with age appropriate toys/activities and of course enjoying time on her favorite playground item, the ship slide.

In 2016 Journey participated in the children's ship parade. During this time the staff took the children around the ship and allowed them to perform while singing and marching. It truly blessed our hearts to see her enjoying the cruise with other children. One of our greatest memories was when we returned home and she pulled out a book from her shelf and said, "We read this book at my cruise school." We already knew she had personalized her experience.

On some ships there are characters on board for children. Throughout the ship the characters participate in activities such as singing, dancing, parades, ice and aqua shows giving the children a memorable time. Family time is also offered. During these times games, talent shows, and events are offered to gather families together. In need of a date night on the waves? No worries! Babysitting services are offered for late night activities throughout the ship.

So you may be thinking, "That sounds great for young children but what about my teenage son or daughter?" No worries! There are several activities, dance clubs, arcades, entertainment and teen only spots geared to accommodate them. They won't miss social media with the agenda the cruise provides.

Cruises offer something for everyone. Whether or not you bring along children you will be amazed at how accommodating this experience is. The entire family can enjoy the wide variety of family-friendly activities on and off the ship. The quality time, fond memories and new experiences provide priceless opportunities that you'll never regret.

It just brings tears to our eyes when we share our story on how our cruise-time blesses each of us individually and as family. We spend countless nights reminiscing about funny stories or pictures that we all share. Most of all we are blessed to know that at the age of four Journey loves her cruise experience just as much as her parents. We birthed a cruiser!

Chapter 10

Waves of Financial Preparation

Our excitement about the cruise experience is always high, but it is especially high in the first few weeks after we return from the cruise. Upon our return home to our family and friends, of course we love to share the pictures and stories from our cruise vacation. As we give our loved ones the details of our wonderful days at sea, we remind them that they too should go and experience the cruise for themselves. However, a very common response is, "I am not sure I am financially able to take such a vacation."

We truly understand that life presents every person with a fair share of responsibilities and financial obligations. Mortgage, rent, bills, groceries, and other basic necessities of life must definitely take precedence in the budgeting of one's money. However, bear in mind that the "daily grind" of taking care of such responsibilities can take a toll on a person mentally, emotionally and physically if he or she does not take the time to get refreshed once in a while. Very early on in our marriage, we realized that getting such a refreshing at least once a year is of the utmost importance. Upon reading the previous chapters of this book, you can see that our yearly cruise vacation provides the perfect refreshing for us. It helps us to "detox" from the stress and pressure the previous year may have provided. For this reason, the cruise is a necessary part of our lives and therefore we make sure it is a part of our yearly budget.

We would like to encourage you with a few pointers that may help make your cruise vacation financially possible. Whether your annual income is "six figures" or whether it is much less than that, you should expect to be financially able to go on a cruise vacation.

The first thing you must do (if you don't do so already) is to write down a budget. It is usually best to prepare a monthly budget. In addition to writing down your anticipated income for the month, you should write down your anticipated bills and expenses. Since you will be saving for a cruise, write down an anticipated amount you will set aside for the cruise. The cost of cruises range from about $300.00 per person (for some of the shorter cruises) to about $1,100.00 per person (for some of the longer cruises). Of course, the cost increases if you desire the more luxurious suites on the ships. If you live far away from the cruise ports, you may want to factor in an extra $300.00 or so per person for travel from your home to the port. Use these estimated amounts to calculate how much you need to save per month to have enough for the cruise at the designated time.

We teach an introductory budgeting class at our church, and one of the main points of our lesson is "Making Small Changes Adds Up." There is a possibility that, throughout your week, you may be spending a few unnecessary dollars on various things. Perhaps you go out to a restaurant for lunch every day. Assuming the average restaurant lunch costs $7.00, you probably spend at least $35.00 each week for lunch. If you bring your lunch from home, you would only spend about $15.00 per week for the items you need to prepare your lunch daily. If you bring your lunch from home instead of going to the restaurant every day, you could save $20.00 or more each week! Each week, set aside the $20.00 in your own personal "savings" for your cruise. (Of course, this should be written down in your budget.) With that approach, you can easily save over $1,000.00 within a year!

Think about other small changes you can make in your spending habits. Perhaps, instead of buying individual chips or candy bars at a vending machine daily, you can buy those items in bulk. Calculate the amount you save by buying in bulk, and add it to your cruise savings. If you really brainstorm, you can find ways to curb costs. Some people don't realize how often they get their hair styled (or cut), how often they take clothes to the cleaners, how often they go to the movies, etc. You will be amazed how you are able to save up!

We often call our billing companies (for our cell phone bill, internet bill, electric bill, gas bill, water bill etc.) to find out how we can cut a few dollars from those bills. Sometimes we learn of "special rates" on our phone and internet bills when we call, or we learn of tips to keep the electric, gas and water bills from going too high. All of these things save us money. We compare grocery stores, and we know which items cost less at which grocery stores and we shop accordingly. This saves us hundreds of dollars each month. Moreover, we are very careful and prayerful about what else we spend our money on. We stick to our budget as closely as possible. Sometimes we have to say "no" to certain entertainment or recreational activities we would normally enjoy, so that we can say "yes" to the cruise!

As a side note, we are givers! We love to give generously to our church, to other worthy causes, and to those who are in need. It is amazing how our generosity always returns to us in a greater measure – many times in the form of unexpected money!

When you truly make up your mind that you WILL go on the cruise, when you write down your financial plan for the cruise in your budget, and when you follow your budget without compromise, you will surely find yourself booking that cruise in the very near future!

Chapter 11

Waves of Good-Byes

We've had the time of our lives! The night before leaving the ship is always bitter sweet. We've had time to relax and unwind. On that night, we reflect on the laughter and the great times that we've shared. We usually just sit on the balcony and discuss the new memories of our vacation week while also discussing our vision for the year ahead of us. We reflect on what God has brought us through and what He is preparing us for. We marvel at how we beheld the wonders of His creation while visiting parts of the world that we had previously only heard or read about. At that time we always reiterate how thankful we are that we followed our coworker's recommendation. We laugh at the thought of all we would have missed if we would have given in to our initial fears about the cruise. We reminisce on how much we enjoyed being in the middle of the Caribbean (or the Atlantic, or the Mediterranean) with so much to do! We express our awe of the fact that on such huge ships we hardly ever feel any significant rocking or swaying (thanks to their powerful stabilizers). In all of our years of cruising, neither of us have ever experienced motion sickness! It brings sadness to know that in the morning we will have to say goodbye. However, we're quickly filled with joy and happiness because we know that, by the grace of God, we'll be returning.

The last morning is different. The ship is quiet and everyone is in the dining area eating their last buffet-style breakfast. Everyone has the same look on their faces - "I just need one more day!" Everyone is dressed in normal attire ready to go to the airport or to their vehicles in order to head to their various places of residence.

Since we are among thousands of passengers who must exit the ship in an orderly fashion, we are assigned a specific place to meet just prior to our designated time to disembark. Once we are off of the ship, we proceed to customs. We then gather our luggage and step onto the airport transfer where we're greeted with the same friendly smiles as when we arrived. Usually everyone just sits back and listens to the driver who gives information about where we are and where we are headed. Once we arrive at the airport our luggage is handed back to us and we prepare for our flight back home.

Shortly after you leave the cruise port, it is likely that you will receive an email from the cruise line wishing you a safe trip back home. You may also receive a survey from the cruise line at that time so that you can provide feedback. The cruise line loves to know that your cruise experience was all that you had hoped it to be. Hours later you will likely receive an email from the cruise line welcoming you back home. Yes! Even on the trip back home you continue to receive the same excellent service that you received while booking and cruising. Long after you return to "life on the land", the wonders of your cruise vacation will surely replay in your mind. Wave by wave, the memories will overflow. Though your family life may be centered at 123 Main Street for the majority of the year, you will long for the day that you can return for another cruise and say as the Stallworths say,

"HOME SWEET HOME"!

Waves from the Heart

I Love Cruisin'

I Love Cruisin.....never thought I'd say it; I was hesitant to go on my first cruise at the age of 56 years young! I was talked into it by a dear friend and now I'm a cruiser for life! Sailing the seas creates a vacation that allows you rest, relaxation, adventure, fun, restoration and supplies you with endless stories to tell of your experience on the cruise and wonderful memories to forever hold with you. On the cruise you are treated like "Royalty," all the crew members are so attentive and really know how to take care of their guests. I highly recommend getting a room with a balcony, to be able to sit on that balcony and overlook the ocean as you sail endless miles, you are engulfed in such peace and serenity! Our lives get so busy and cruisin gives you that restoration that you need at least once a year, you don't have to think about anything, everything is done for you all you have to do is get up and decide what you want for that day, whether it is an excursion on one of the islands that you port at, or laying by the pool all day long enjoying the sunshine and refreshing pool, it's all up to you! Let your dreams set sail...

Colleen, age 58

#CruisingIs4Me

I have had the pleasure of enjoying four (4) voyages on cruise ships which were literally "cities on the sea." My very first cruise was forty years ago, and unfortunately, I only remember a few things...getting my finger slammed in the car door in the way to the port (that really hurt), the family who joined us on our sailing experience, donning our FORMAL DUDS to meet the captain, and Flaming Alaska (I had never seen a dessert served ON FIRE before!) Because my other cruises were taken within the last eleven years, I am able to recall more details. With each "Bon Voyage", the cruise experience became increasingly more enjoyable and intriguing! I have enjoyed the dessert & coffee café, on-board shops, wonderful cuisine (including the midnight buffet,) and the interactive games. Each excursion was rich and rewarding as I met new people, enjoyed wonderful shows, and took souvenir pictures. Oh, yes! The ports of call...each island destination had its own culture and a plethora of souvenirs from which to choose. Where else can one be called "pretty lady" everywhere she goes except when she tries to ignore the Island Vendors? I felt that the most special part of each cruise was witnessing the handiwork of God and understanding more fully the scripture that states, "For the earth shall be filled with the knowledge of the glory of the LORD, as the waters cover the sea." Habakkuk 2:14....FILL ME UP, LORD! (With your knowledge and with that good food!) #CruisingIs4Me

Genene, age 50

Cruising...

Throughout my lifetime I have traveled to many destinations in the US and abroad, and nothing compares to the joy I've experienced while on a cruise. First and foremost is the relaxation and pampering by the cruise staff. Where else can you wake up to and unobstructed sunrise, and go to a white tablecloth breakfast as you plan the rest of your day. We (me and my fiancé) usually do a light workout after relaxing by the pool, on non excursion days, then enjoy a healthy lunch. As for the entertainment, we make it a point to see a nightly show every night as we are already dressed from attending a semi or formal dinner. We also manage to get out on the deck to watch, the also amazing unobstructed sunset. All of this is done on a one week cruise (times can vary) while visiting amazing "ports of call" where we have experienced unique customs and incredible sites. We have enjoyed cruising so much that we have decided to exchange vowels on our next cruise. Never say never again, especially if you cruise together...

Michael & Charmaine, ages 50 and 53

Cruising

Cruising has made exploring the world a lot more interesting and a lot more fun. From the moment we start boarding all the way to customs, from the never ending food to all the different shows, all the different activities and all the different people. Cruising has also opened my eyes to more cultural diversity. Not just with going to different countries and experiencing their lifestyles but just being on the ship with all different walks of life, getting to meet new people from far and wide and becoming one big melting pot for a series of days. The staff is another one of my favorite parts about cruising. They make my stay so much more enjoyable, they get to know me and they're always so sweet and willing to make sure everyone is happy. I like that we get to choose if we want to get up and go to a show, go eat or decide if we want to stay in our rooms all day and order room service. Just being able to relax and have no care. Freedom is the best way to spend a vacation.

Zoe, age 20

The Ship

The places were fun. Can we go again because it is fun? The ship was very big and I loved the waters, I loved everything that the school teachers did. The food was so good and I wonder if we could go again. The pilot took us far in the water; the bunk bed was very big and normal. I know people loved the shows and jokes. I want people to go because they never went. The ship was amazing and I felt good because we had so much fun on the ship because it was bigger than our whole house. My favorite part was the dancing on ice because I've never seen it before. The people who worked on the ship were nice because they spoke to the children, so children should come.

Journey, age 4

Stallworth Family

Kevin, Latoya
&
Journey

July 7, 2015 ... Enjoying 8 years of cruising!

Cruising has become such a part of our lives that everyone asks us right after we return, "Where are you going next year?"

We are loyal to the waves!

Contact us at: wavesofwonder@yahoo.com